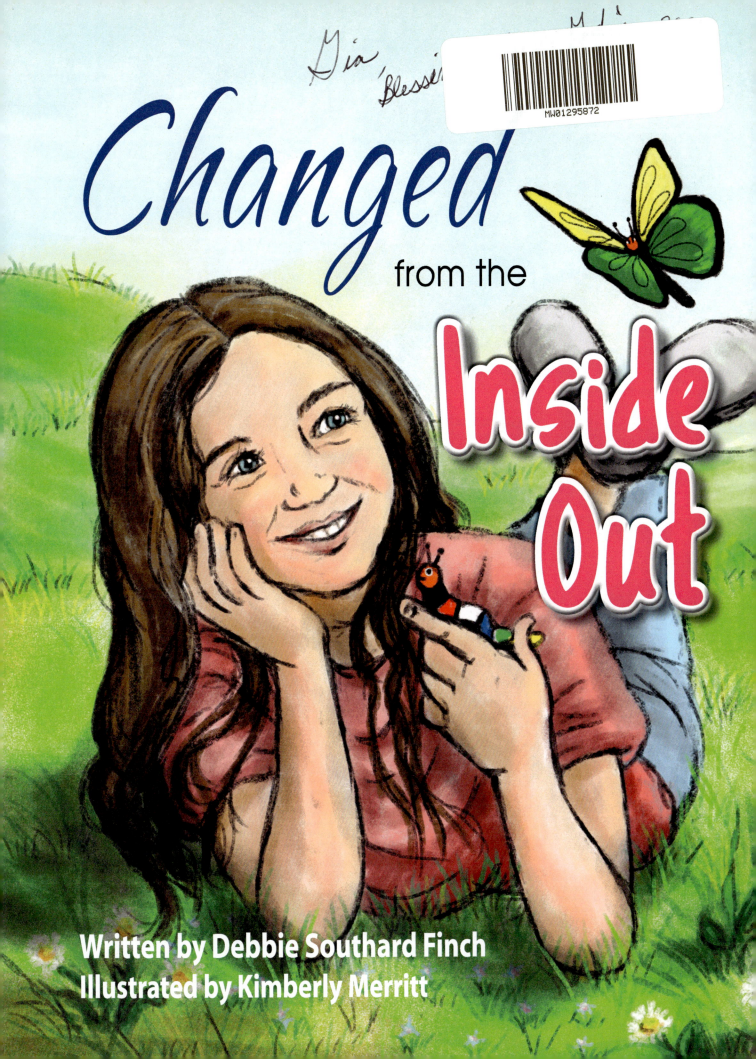

I would like to thank the following individuals for their love and support throughout the writing and publishing of ***Changed from the Inside Out:***
Belinda Hurley, Jim Southard, Pat Southard, Suzanne Southard, and Betsy Stivers.
My dear family and friends, I love you more than you will ever know. I thank God for inspiring me to write this book. I pray it will touch and change many lives for Jesus.

Whenever I think of a **CATERPILLAR** and the stages it goes through to become a *butterfly,* it reminds me of how God changes us.

A caterpillar crawls inch by inch all day long, hunting and looking for food he needs to survive.

Then the caterpillar climbs a vine and refuses to eat another bite. He hangs upside down from a branch and spins a warm, silky cocoon or molts into a shiny chrysalis. This becomes his temporary home—the place where his TRANSFORMATION begins. The caterpillar digests itself and releases special enzymes that liquefy his tissues.

He is now "caterpillar soup" and sleeps for weeks. When his long nap is over, he wakes up and is very uncomfortable. He wishes someone would help him. God helps him by forming him into a **new insect**.

We too are changed by what we go through in this life. When we give our lives to the Lord, we become a **new creation**. Old things are gone. The new has come.

This bound insect can't get very far in life because he moves so slowly and cannot see the big plan God has for him. God created this *amazing creature* and has a beautiful future for him, but there needs to be some changes. Change can be hard, but the caterpillar refuses to stay the same. He wants to be different and be completely changed.

Just because we become a Christian doesn't mean we always see what is best for us. Many times we would choose an easier way, but God always sees the big picture. So we must **TRUST HIM** for our future.

The caterpillar's body slowly begins to change while in his cocoon. He knows God only desires what is best for him.

Sometimes we don't want to change, even when we see others growing and changing. But we must remember God only wants what is **best for our lives.**

The caterpillar knows the process is worth the struggle. He is ready for a big change.

What we think is a difficult struggle can actually be a metamorphosis. *God* wants to change us for the better. He desires to *make us the best version* of ourselves we could ever become.

When the transformation is complete, the *butterfly* breaks out of the chrysalis and flaps his colorful wings.

Sometimes *blessings* come in disguise. Difficulties can change us for the better and **make us more like Jesus.** We might even think our lives are over and will never be the same. Troubles can make us bitter or better. We can emerge from the dark, hard places of life like a beautiful butterfly.

A butterfly's beautiful wings carry him in the sky, where he can test his wings and explore his surroundings.

We too will be tested as we discover **GOD'S WILL** for our lives.

A butterfly is not just an insect; it is a symbol and a sign of the miraculous changes God can make in each of our lives. The little creature is determined to find his purpose in life. One special day God touched him and made a big change.

God can touch us too. He wants to transform us just like He did the caterpillar.

The caterpillar was ready for a big change in his life. When we believe God gave His only Son, Jesus, to save us and forgive us of all the bad things we have ever done, He will make a big change in our lives. He will help us grow and become a beautiful "butterfly" for Him. He

will use us to help other people know Him. Now do you understand why whenever I think of a caterpillar and the stages it goes through to become a butterfly, it reminds me of how Jesus changes us?

Don't forget!

You were ONCE like that caterpillar.

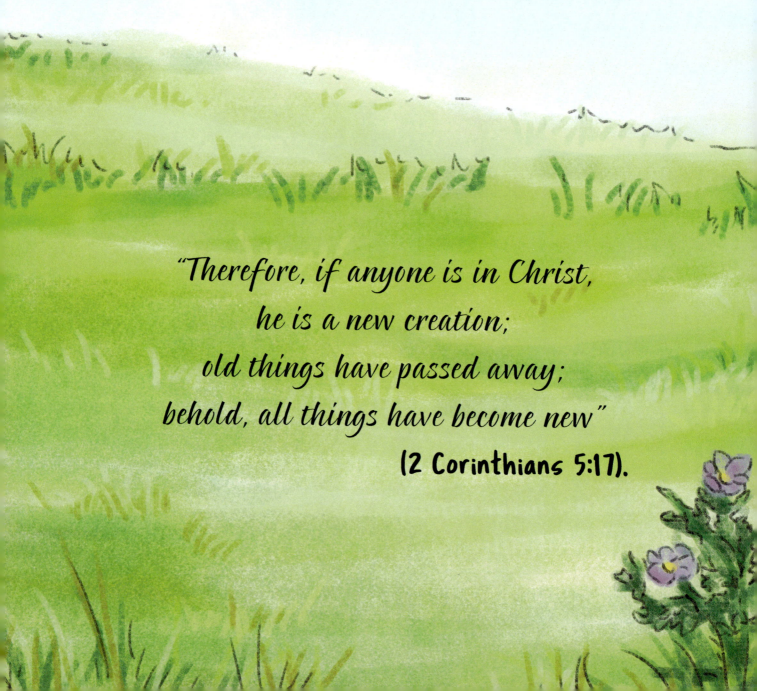

Jesus answered and said to him,
"Most assuredly, I say to you,
unless one is born again,
he cannot see the kingdom of God"
(John 3:3).

"Therefore, if anyone is in Christ,
he is a new creation;
old things have passed away;
behold, all things have become new"
(2 Corinthians 5:17).

Changed from the Inside Out © 2018 by Debbie Southard Finch. All rights reserved. No portion of this book may be reproduced, stored in a retrieval system, or transmitted in any form or by any means, except for brief quotations in printed reviews, without prior permission from the author. Requests for information should be addressed to the author at dfinch@crmail.k12.ar.us.

Scripture quotations are taken from the **New King James Version®**. Copyright © 1982 by Thomas Nelson. Used by permission. All rights reserved.

Illustrations by Kimberly Merritt
Edited by ChristianEditingServices.com